# Benson's

# Bad Boys

**Benson, Arizona**

*Mary Lee Tiernan*

*Benson's Bad Boys*

First Paperback Edition
August 2013

ISBN-13: 978-1490939766
ISBN-10: 1490939768

Copyright © 2013 by Mary Lee Tiernan

All rights reserved. No portion of this book may be copied or reproduced in any format without the prior written consent of the author, except in the case of brief quotations used in reviews.

# Benson's

# Bad Boys

# Acknowledgements

Special thanks to the San Pedro Valley Arts & Historical Society (Benson Museum), the Family History Center in Pomerene, Edward Ellsworth, and Bob Nilson, for their assistance in collecting resources used for this project.

The steam engine pictured on the cover and in the interior belonged to the El Paso and Southwestern Railroad, which was one of three major railways to service Benson. Photo courtesy of the San Pedro Valley Arts & Historical Society.

The westward movement of the 1800s brought countless people to the West, especially after the Civil War. Construction of the transcontinental railroads truly opened the land for settlement. Trains provided safer passage because they were not as prone to the Indian and highwaymen attacks that plagued stagecoaches and wagons. And the swiftness of train travel shortened the otherwise grueling journey westward.

Southern Pacific Railroad constructed a railway from California to Texas. Workers left Yuma, California in 1877 to lay track across the Arizona and New Mexico Territories to connect with the Texas and Pacific Railway in El Paso, Texas. When the two railroads met, the rails would form one continuous line from coast to coast across the southern U.S. A good day yielded two more miles of track. Year by year, the ribbon of steel stretched farther and farther across the desert. Workers finally reached the San Pedro Valley, where Geronimo and his band of Apaches still roamed and terrorized settlers and travelers.

On June 14, 1880, Southern Pacific reached the site chosen for crossing the San Pedro River. The site was just south of the crossing once used by the Butterfield Overland Stagecoach Company. The Butterfield line had been discontinued 19 years earlier in 1861, but stagecoaches and wagons traveling east or west still used the old Butterfield route and crossing. By the first week of July, the construction crews had erected a bridge across the river and added three more miles of track eastward. The workers would continue on, but leave behind a new town.

On the west side of the river near the crossing, Southern Pacific built a town it named Benson. The San Pedro Valley had functioned as a natural north/south corridor for centuries. Francisco Vázquez de Coronado, for example, used the corridor in the 1500s when he traveled north from Mexico to find the legendary Seven Cities of Gold. The intersection at the northern end of the corridor at Benson was ideal for a railhead. Not only would the railroad provide service along its east/west route, but it would also service the towns and ranches that dotted the landscape to the north and south.

A frenzy of prospecting throughout the West, including the San Pedro Valley, had begun in 1848 with the discovery of gold in California. Three years before the founding of Benson, Ed Schiefflin had discovered silver in Tombstone. Miners flocked to the area and filed numerous claims for their share of the wealth. The mining industry was about to explode in the region after the discovery of copper and the founding of Bisbee in 1880. Minerals were also discovered in numerous smaller mines all around the area.

Towns sprang up overnight at the news of a strike; many died just as quickly. Mining towns often began as 'tent cities.' Tents were later replaced by small frame 'moveable' houses without foundations. They were built in sections, so they could be assembled and disassembled when their owners heard of a new strike and moved to the next location. They simply took their houses with them because building materials were not always easily accessible in the Southwest desert.

Benson carved its existence out of bare land, much as the mining towns did. The *Weekly Arizona Citizen* reported on July 10, 1880, that the "Town is very lively just now, and already there are thought to be about 300 people there, while a hotel, three restaurants, six or seven saloons, five or six stores, and two livery stables are doing a 'land-office business.' This growth was nearly all accomplished inside of two weeks."[1] Most of these early wood-framed buildings were not very substantial, although perhaps a step-up from mining towns like Tombstone and Bisbee which started out as 'tent cities.' Benson had the advantage of the train bringing building materials right to its doorstep.

Laying railroad tracks across the desert. Photo courtesy of the San Pedro Valley Arts & Historical Society

Wild behavior in the streets was not uncommon in Benson's early days. After all, the Old West thrived in the southeastern Arizona Territory during the late 1880s and early 1900s due to the combination of rough living conditions, a lack of sufficient numbers of law enforcers, and the temporary status of most town dwellers. Fear of Indian attacks, shootouts, cowboys, saloons, hangings, fights: all the images one conjures up of the Wild West could be found in Benson.

Benson's population its first year hovered around 300 comprised mostly of railroad workers, cowboys, and miners. It was a predominantly male and transient population. As the population grew through the decade, it continued to be primarily male. In four years, the population of Benson doubled; in thirty years, it quadrupled.

That the population was transient is important. Transients were not interested in the growth of a town or in settling down or in becoming law-abiding citizens. They came temporarily for an opportunity and would move on. In the meanwhile, they'd just whoop it up and have a good time. Their behavior gave rise to the reputation of the Wild West. "...in 1882 it (Benson) was an all-night place with 13 saloons. There were eight livery stables, and they had to pile wood up on the side to keep the bullets out. There were forty trains through here every night. It was the biggest station on the S.P. road."[2]

Whether railroad worker, miner, or cowboy, a man gets mighty thirsty after a hard day's labor. He needs a cool drink and a little entertainment, which explains the popularity and existence of so many saloons. Entertainment in a saloon centered around gambling, commonly a game of cards or roulette. Gambling in those days was not illegal and was an accepted activity among men. The combination of liquor, cheating, and sore losers, however, led to many a fistfight or gunplay. But the liquor and gambling weren't always enough for a lonely, single man wanting female companionship in a predominantly male population. And so came one more business in addition to the saloons.

Although prostitution was not exactly legal in early Arizona, laws against it were generally not enforced either. "Madams were often fined to keep the respectable citizens of the towns happy, but the amounts were usually small and more often than not, the city officials were regular customers. The fact is that prostitutes in the Old West were

4th Street or Main Street in the early 1900s. Photo courtesy of the San Pedro Valley Arts & Historical Society

good for the economy of a town and brought in money. So while respectable women crossed the street and refused to acknowledge the prostitutes, they were helping to add to a town's coffers and attracting new inhabitants to the area."[3] In Tombstone, no one bothered the girls as long as they bought a business license. "Revenue collected from the sale of these licenses was, for many years, the sole source of financial support for Tombstone's schools. Although considered to be a profession of sin, large contributions helped to build area churches, and during times of illness, the parlor houses not only housed the sick, but the girls provided their care."[4]

In mining and railroad towns, the brothel operated as a place of entertainment. The brothel in Benson on the northeast side of town near Gila and Second Street functioned the same way. It offered a dance hall, gambling tables, and a bar as well as the services of young women. "This bawdyhouse was the swingingest place in town. The tinny clinking of the piano, high-pitched laughter interspersed with loud hoot and hollers let the folks on main street know that business was open for another day. Although the house was some distance from downtown, voices and music carried easily to the merchants and patrons on the other side of the railroad tracks."[5]

Lawlessness ruled Benson's earliest years despite efforts to establish law and order. Historian Edward Ellsworth compiled Coroner Inquest Reports from 1881 to 1889 for people buried in the 7th Street Cemetery. Of those he found, shootings account for 63% of the deaths. Only half of those identify the shooter. Of course, not all of these records deal with unlawful activity. Railroad accidents caused a number of deaths. Rafaela Disonra died of "excessive" old age. He was 80.

But not one of the inquest reports mentions hanging. Death by hanging was the West's answer to swift 'justice,' often carried out by vigilantes, citizens who sometimes

Southern Pacific train station in the 1880s
Photo courtesy of Edward Ellsworth

reacted in the heat of the moment more from tempers, liquor, or prejudice than from investigation of the facts. Otherwise stable, law-abiding citizens simply 'had enough' and took the law into their own hands to rid the town of undesirables. In such cases, once done, it was not talked about and no official records existed of the executions.

In August of 1881, a gunfight erupted in Benson involving the Top and Bottom Gang. So notorious was their reputation as thieves and highwaymen that the *Arizona Weekly Citizen* commented, "Better the unfortunate victims of these men be in the hands of the Apaches than in the clutches of this gang."[6] A dispute over a game of cards initially led to a fistfight between Ed Byrnes and Mart (Chuck) Maloney. But on day two of the disagreement, they brought out the pistols.

Byrnes and Maloney fired at each other and missed. One of Byrnes's bullets, however, accidently hit Deputy Sheriff Hiram McComus as he approached the two to stop the gunplay. The bullet hit McComus in the leg and he fell to the ground. Several citizens carried the deputy into a nearby house, then chased down Byrnes yelling about a lynching. "There was a rumor last evening that Byrnes, of the top and bottom game notoriety (sic), had been lynched at Benson, but the news was too good to be true..."[7]

Deputy Sheriff William Breckenridge of Tombstone happened to be in Benson when Byrnes shot McComus. He arrested the gunman and took him into custody. Byrnes was charged with "assault to commit murder on Deputy Sheriff McComus," but was later "discharged from custody"[8] after examination by a Court Commissioner.

Byrnes's arrest did not appease the townsfolk. Immediately after his arrest, they took all the furniture out of the saloon the gang frequented and burned it in the street. "The gang was invited to leave town before sundown and promised a necktie party in their honor if they remained. The outlaws took a train for Tucson that evening."[9] The Top and Bottom Gang got off with a warning. Not all outlaws, or suspected outlaws, were so lucky.

4th Street and Huachuca circa 1912

The corner building with its distinctive diagonal door still exists. It has housed numerous different businesses over the years.

Photo courtesy of the
San Pedro Valley Arts & Historical Society

Some people believe myths, and repeat them as fact. Such is the case when someone claims that paddleboats used to navigate the San Pedro River. The Colorado River, yes; the San Pedro, no. The San Pedro is not, and never was, wide enough or deep enough for a paddleboat. On the other hand, generations of Bensonites treated the story of Los Triaditos, "the castoffs," as merely a myth. It isn't.

Again in the early 1880s, probably 1882 or 1883, three Mexicans, Los Triaditos, met their end in a lumber yard without benefit of trial, without any record of their names or their deaths. Had it not been for the Mexican community, the victims would have faded into oblivion.

Two of the Mexicans were accused of attempting a train robbery, the third of horse-stealing. Since local mesquite trees are too short and flexible for hangings, vigilantes marched them to the local lumber yard and hanged them from a crossbeam.

Once the noose had completed its work, their bodies were taken off the gallows and put into wood coffins. Locals refused to allow their burial in the cemetery, considered to be hallowed ground and not fitting for outlaws. Instead, they were buried outside the south end of the cemetery, across an arroyo under a mesquite tree. Two wood crosses marked their graves for many years.

The Mexican Catholic community believed their souls went to limbo, a place between Heaven and Hell for the lost or forgotten. Only by helping those still on earth could these souls redeem themselves and enter Heaven. So the community began visiting their graves, tending to them, and leaving candles as a symbol of their prayers and wishes. As late as World War I, candles flickered through the night, candle drippings adorned the tree branches, and broken shards of candle holders littered the ground.

Years passed and the tradition faded. The wood crosses rotted and disappeared. The Mexican community no longer visited the graves. No more candles flickered in the night. People forgot.

Local historians questioned whether or not there was any truth to the story. Elizabeth Brenner, representative of Benson's Historical Preservation Commission, her husband Don, and local historians Edward Ellsworth and Vay Fenn decided to find out. So on April 4 and 5, 2008, they went to

Bones of Los Triaditos uncovered
Photo courtesy of Edward Ellsworth

the burial site, and Vay Fenn began excavating with his backhoe. At six feet, finding nothing, they began to despair. But knowing that fill had been added to the arroyo over the years, they kept digging. Eight feet down, they found bones.

The wood coffins had long since deteriorated, but the nails that once held them together remained. Two of the bodies had been buried head to foot in one coffin; the third body, its head missing, in another. Carefully, the historians collected the bones and put them into three containers.

They then dug a grave for each man inside the south wall of the 7th St. Cemetery, just across the arroyo from their original burial site, and re-interred the bones. History has hidden the men's names, their guilt or innocence shall never be proved or disproved, but at least after more than 125 years, their new, marked graves in the cemetery attest to their existence and violent deaths.

Typical of the Old Wild West and a transient male population which had little respect for the law and few lawmen to enforce it, arguments were settled with guns. "Back in 1887, Benson was still a raw western town and law was carried in a man's pocket..."[10] One responded to threats with a gun.

Sometimes gunplay erupted when the boys were just whooping it up and having fun. The editor of the *Tombstone Epitaph* in covering news about Benson in 1882 said, "Last evening some of the 'boys' got to shooting at the 'stars,' but as I am not in communication with those planets I can't say whether or not anybody up there was killed."[11]

"Benson as well as the miner's camps was in those early days rather 'wild and wooly.' There were saloons and

The East Benson train station. Photo courtesy of the San Pedro Valley Arts & Historical Society

gambling galore and the few people who lived 'in town' found it prudent to stay in their houses at night if they did not wish to take the chance of stopping stray bullets."[12]

In 1880, when Jacob and Lizzie Trask and their daughter Laura arrived in Benson, they first stayed with their friends, the Kittridge family, until they could locate housing.

"The first afternoon —quite late, near sundown—they heard shouting and shooting. Mama (Laura Trask) ran to the front door and stepped outside. Almost at that same moment some 'characters' rode by shouting and firing their six-guns. Mrs. Kittridge grabbed mother and jerked her back inside where she gave the young lady quite a dressing down. Mother felt a jolt at her feet before Mrs. K grabbed her. The next morning they were out in front and found a bullet hole in the riser of the step mother was standing on."[13]

In March 1906, Harry Fisher "while on a spree shot up the town of Benson and was compelled by Justice Titus to contribute the sum of $100 to the county treasury."[14] One of his bullets went through a window in the Southern Pacific Depot hitting a lamp on one of the tables, narrowly missing a clerk at work in the office.

"...during gunfights, (it is) rumored that Leonard Redfield, postmaster at the time, would put his wife inside the door of the safe to protect her from flying lead."[15]

Out on the range, justice was also meted out with a gun. For rustlers, according to rancher Gerry McGoffin, "They'd just be shot. There wouldn't be a trial or anything. They'd just be shot."[16]

The slightest displeasure could trigger gun use, as in the case of Charlie Henricksen or Henderson, depending on the source. Railroads often shared their water supply with the residents of small towns, whether from a cistern, a tank car, or a well. In Benson's case, it was a well. Southern Pacific had dug a deep well to provide water for their train locomotives. Residents who had not dug their own wells went to the pump house for buckets of water for domestic use.

Charlie Henricksen was in charge of the pump house in East Benson. He particularly liked the pretty Mexican ladies who came for buckets of water and charged each of them a kiss as payment for the water. No kiss, no water. The ladies may not have been as happy with the arrangement as Charlie was. In April 1884, Ciprano Cruz went to the pump

Our Lady of Lourdes Catholic Church in East Benson circa 1894. Photo courtesy of Edward Ellsworth from the Mejia family collection.

Note the vacant space surrounding the church and compare to the next photograph taken a decade later.

house himself. "Charlie saw his cozy arrangement threatened and refused to serve the man. Cruz tried to take the water, but Henderson became irate and shot and killed him."[17]. Henricksen was arrested.

This case has been cited as an example of the racial prejudice that existed in early Benson. While Anglos and Hispanics united in the neighboring community of Tres Alamos against their common enemy—the Apaches—the development of an Anglo town offered no such unifying factor. It is doubtful Charlie would ever have demanded a kiss from white women coming to the pump house. The community or Southern Pacific would have stopped him. He felt safe, however, in extorting sexual favors from Hispanic women.

East Benson in the early 1900s. Photo Courtesy of Edward Ellsworth.
Note the cross on the church spire and the development
of East Benson since the previous photo.

The railroad usually had trouble from outlaws, not from their own employees. One night in 1881, a Wells, Fargo & Co. stage carrying bars of silver bullion drove up to the depot platform to unload. "While the messenger was taking them into the building, necessitating his absence from the platform only for a few seconds at a time, some person or persons got away with one of the bars, valued in the neighborhood of $2,000. Diligent search was immediately made but no clue has been found, as yet, to the daring robbers. Wells, Fargo & Co. offer a reward of $450 for the recovery of the bullion and $300 each for the parties implicated in any way to the theft."[18]

The Hotel Arnold built in 1906 still stands but is in deplorable condition.
It is the only surviving hotel from Benson's early days.
Photo courtesy of the San Pedro Valley Arts & Historical Society.

Another incident took place at the Benson railroad yard in 1882 which prompted the *Tombstone Epitaph* to say: "The industrious scoundrels, who are rapidly earning an unenviable reputation for the town of Benson, added another to their long list of outrages and crimes..."[19]

Railroad workers left two passenger cars on the track a couple of hundred feet back from the station while the railroad switched cars. Busy at their tasks, the workers were unaware that robbers had entered the unguarded cars.

"Four of the scoundrels stood at each of the four doors and with pistols in hand commanded silence. The rest of the robbers then ransacked the two cars and took everything of value that could be found, even going as far as taking gold rings and jewelry from women and young girls. One old woman who was traveling to California with her two daughters had a purse containing $270 forcefully taken from her clinched hand; an old man had a pair of fine boots taken off his feet, and three young girls who were sleeping in a corner of one of the cars were robbed of their bedding. It took about fifteen minutes to complete the job, and the robbers absconded and have not been heard of since."[20]

These are only two sample incidents of criminal activity in the railroad yards. The railroad hired its own police to handle unlawful problems on their property.

Hobos 'riding the rails' posed another constant problem and sometimes caused fatal accidents when they missed their footing jumping on and off the trains. The hobos most often gained access to the trains as they slowed down at the bridge rather than in the yard itself.

The Tombstone reporter who wrote about the above incident spoke of Benson "rapidly earning an unenviable reputation." Benson with its population of 300 could not compete with Tombstone's 15,000 for the title of Wildest Town in the West. In the early 1880s, 92 saloons lined Allen Street, the main street in Tombstone.

A quote used earlier by resident William Ohnesorgen claimed Benson had 13 saloons in 1882. "...in 1882 it (Benson) was an all-night place with 13 saloons." A report in the *Tombstone Epitaph* in 1882, however, says nine.[21] The discrepancy may be caused by how a saloon was defined—whether as a stand-alone business or whether bars in restaurants and the brothel were included.

4th Street also called Front Street or Main Street
Photo courtesy of Edward Ellsworth

The Bird Cage Theatre in Tombstone, perched at the east end of Allen Street, offered a man all types of pleasures as a saloon, theatre, gambling hall, and brothel. The pleasures went on day or night, seven days a week, until it closed in 1889. While Benson had its house of ill-repute, it never earned a reputation as the "wildest, wickedest night spot between Basin Street and the Barbary Coast,"[22] as the Bird Cage did from the New York Times. Nor did it have an alleged 140 bullet holes found in the walls and ceiling.

During its heyday, Tombstone had earned a bad reputation for too much gun play and too many shootings. But no shootout has ever matched the saga of what happened on October 26, 1881 at the O.K. Corral between the Earps and the Cowboys. Those 30 shots in 24 seconds have generated almost a century and a half of discussion and controversy.

Benson's most famous shootout occurred on Thanksgiving Day in 1906. The Fashion Saloon, formerly the Wildcat Saloon, was crowded. According to the customers, proprietor Harry K. Fisher had been quarreling with his bartender Jack McCullough all evening. As midnight approached, "...before anyone realized what was going on each of the parties to the dispute had whipped out a gun and started shooting."[23]

In the space of a minute, McCullough, using an old style Colt revolver, fired three shots. One shot hit Fisher in the hip. Fisher, using the new Colt automatic, fired six shots. All six hit the bartender. Witnesses said McCullough fired first and Fisher only returned fire after McCullough had shot at him several times.

When the shooting stopped, the crowd scattered to find a physician and an officer. Arizona Ranger Lieutenant Harry Wheeler happened to be close to the saloon and heard the shots. He arrived as the crowd dispersed. Wheeler arrested Fisher, who turned over his gun without any resistance. A physician arrived, pronounced McCullough dead, and tended to Fisher's wound.

Fisher was held without bail until the district attorney conducted a preliminary examination of the case on December 8th. "It is the consensus of opinion that he will be restored to liberty on the ground that he had to shoot to protect his life."[24]

But he wasn't freed at the preliminary hearing. Fisher was later granted bail in the amount of $2,500. By December 13th, Fisher still sat in jail awaiting delivery of his bail to the clerk's office in Tombstone. He also waited for the grand jury to convene and decide what, if any, charges he might face for killing McCullough.

View of Benson from the water tower 1903
Photo courtesy of Edward Ellsworth

This story is Benson's most famous shootout because of the stories written about it in future years. It is also a good example of the difficulties in writing a history. Information for the version of the story given above is taken from newspaper articles written at the time of the incident. Newspapers are considered a fairly reliable source. However, even newspapers with a good reputation for factual reporting have reporters who embellish stories and/or do not get their facts straight. A case in point: In the coverage of this shooting, some articles from the *Bisbee Daily Review* gives the bartender's name as P. McCollum. Other articles in the same newspaper, however, use the name Jack McCullough. One article included information about the bartender's bad reputation and his nickname of Jack the Ripper. Testimony by eye-witnesses is not always reliable either—ask any policeman who hears varying versions of the same event.

A dramatic incident appeals to writers of historical events who years later take the basic facts and add details or conclusions to make a story more colorful. Were those added details the result of research or did the writer fictionalize the story? Based on numerous retellings about this shooting, a more colorful version goes something like this. Note that even the names change.

Benson's most famous shootout occurred on Thanksgiving Day in 1906. Train after train brought passengers to town. Many of these passengers were bound for points south, but a strike in Sonora stranded all Mexico-bound trains. With nothing else to do, and with the Wildcat conveniently located just across the street from the depot, the male passengers headed for the saloon.

The Wildcat offered not only drinking, but gambling at the roulette wheel and card tables, a pot-bellied stove for warmth, saloon girls for entertainment, and someone occasionally banging out a tune on the old piano. If the scene sounds like the perfect setting for a western movie, it was, only it was real, and the drinking, gambling, and tempers would lead to the most infamous shootout in Benson's history.

Jack the Ripper worked for Jessie Fisher, owner of the Wildcat. Twas a strange handle Jack had chosen for himself, but in those days, no one questioned why—or knew his real name. His experience as a bartender, roulette croupier, and card dealer was all Jessie needed to know. That Thanksgiving morning, Jack worked the roulette wheel, and by 1:00 p.m. when they closed the saloon for a few hours to eat their holiday dinner, Jessie counted roulette profits of $612, the equivalent of almost $16,100 in 2012. Jessie pocketed $600, and handed Jack $12 as a tip, a tip of less than two percent. Jack was not pleased with such a small tip and said so. But he shrugged it off, and as the two left to go eat, they chatted amiably. The slight had not yet had time to fester.

Arizona Ranger Harry C. Wheeler

When the bar reopened, the crowd swelled as the cowboys arrived to join the festivities. Jack tended bar during the evening and apparently served himself, as well as the customers, more than a few drinks. As the hours wore on, customers heard him grumbling about Jessie's stinginess. Finally, the rowdiness and booze brought Jack's feelings to a boil.

Jack grabbed his gun and shot out the large ceiling lamp, leaving the bar in semi-darkness. His next shot knocked out the small lamp on the piano. In the darkness, customers scrambled for the door or sought cover. A third shot produced a cry of pain, then a responding volley of bullets.

Silence. The crowd began to edge its way back to the doorway. In the dim light, they saw Jack leaning on the bar. He slowly began to tip backwards, then fell to the floor. Jessie, clutching his buttocks, appeared in the doorway yelling for the doctor.

While Dr. Charles Powell attended to Jessie, he told Arizona Ranger Harry Wheeler that when Jack's third shot hit him, he responded in kind to protect his customers. The on-the-spot inquest cleared Jessie of any wrong-doing. The next day while Jack the Ripper was quietly buried, it was business as usual at the Wildcat, except, of course, for the new bartender.

An earlier saloon shooting on May 2, 1902, did not receive the same notoriety. James Shepard and Charles Livingston (or Livingstone) both worked at the Land Saloon, later renamed the Turf, but they did not get along. Shepard tended bar all night on May 1st, but instead of going to bed after his shift, he "proceeded during the day to load himself with booze..."[25] The liquor and lack of sleep finally took its toll, and Shepard fell asleep at the

The Turf Saloon in the early 1900s
Photo courtesy of Ed Lee

roulette table. Charles Morath picked Shepard up and took him to a bed in a back room where Livingston had been lying. Livingston got up and tried to help Morath put Shepard into the bed.

Only Shepard didn't want to go to bed and resisted. According to Morath, during their struggle with Shepard, Livingston's hand slipped, scratching Shepard's face and drawing a little blood. Livingston and Morath left Shepard in the room, but he didn't stay there for long. Livingston went to the bar, and while the bartender fetched him a bottle of beer, Shepard came out of the back room, walked to the bar and behind it, and picked up the bar's revolver. He stood just opposite Livingston on the other side of bar and fired one fatal shot. Shepard was arrested and charged with murder.

"Those who witnessed the killing and who knew Shepard, say that there was never a more cold-blooded murder... they believe Shepard knew precisely what he was going to do."[26] And the coroner's jury determined that Livingston "died from a gunshot wound inflicted by one James Shepard. We further find that the shooting which caused this death was premeditated and unjustifiable..."[27]

During the trial, Shepard accused Livingston of having beaten him up in the back room and that he acted in self-defense because he was fearful for his life. Shepard's first trial ended in a hung jury. His second trial ended in December 1903 with a "not guilty" verdict.

Westerns popularized many images of the Old West, the inside of the Fashion or Wildcat Saloon being one. Another well-known scene places the sheriff on the main street in town, his gun loaded and ready at his side, challenging the lawbreaker while folks watched from the sidelines. Just a few months after the demise of Jack the Ripper, such a gunfight erupted on the streets of Benson on February 28, 1907. It started out in the stereotypic way, but ended with a twist that made it one of the most unusual gunfights in the annals of the West.

The story actually began in late 1905 when an unnamed brunette in her mid-twenties, tall and shapely,[28] met D.W. Silverton in Nevada. She also met another man in Nevada, J.A. Tracy, shortly thereafter in early 1906. A year

Southern Pacific train station. Photo courtesy of the San Pedro Valley Arts & Historical Society

later, 1907, Tracy was working at Vail Station as an agent for the Helvetia Copper Company. The brunette was in Tucson with Silverton. According to one version of the story, Mr. and "Mrs." Silverton claimed to be married by an itinerant preacher, but had no license. Two men vying for the affections of the same woman spells trouble.

When Tracy heard that the brunette was in Tucson, he went to see her. "...he paid her a visit to offer her a diamond ring. She declined, and Tracy returned to Vail's Station without comment. The next day, however, she received four threatening letters from her frustrated suitor."[29]

Meanwhile, the Silvertons decided to take the train to tour Douglas, Bisbee, and Cananea. When the train stopped at Vail Station, the brunette saw Tracy and identified him to her husband. Silverton jumped from the train and confronted Tracy. Their argument must have infuriated Tracy who tried to climb aboard the rear platform of the departing train, but missed. He caught another train and followed the couple to Benson. "On his way... he informed several parties that he intended to kill the couple on sight."[30]

After arriving in Benson, the Silvertons checked into the Virginia Hotel. While standing on the hotel porch the next morning, with a clear view of the depot, Silverton spied Tracy waiting beside the train bound for Bisbee. He hurried back into the hotel and asked hotel proprietor, Eduardo Castaneda, for a gun. Instead, Casteneda contacted Arizona Ranger Lieutenant Harry Wheeler, who was eating breakfast at the hotel.

Silverton explained to Wheeler that "Tracey had followed them and was waiting for them with a gun in his pocket. This man had threatened to kill them previously, that they wished to leave, but were afraid to go to the train..."[31] While they spoke, a porter of the hotel told Silverton that a man was "laying for him," which confirmed Silverton's story. Silverton asked Wheeler for a gun, but the request was refused again. Instead, Wheeler asked him to point out the man. Silverton identified a man who was walking up and down between the passenger train and a boxcar. Wheeler then told Silverton that he and wife should board the train while he dealt with Tracy.

As Wheeler approached Tracy, Tracy saw the Silvertons exiting the hotel. Cursing, Tracy pulled out his gun, and the sharp report of the revolver shattered the morning calm. Wheeler continued to advance, returning fire from his Colt and demanding that Tracy drop his gun. Bullets volleyed

The Virginia Hotel 1902
Photo courtesy of Bob Nilson

back and forth. Tracy hit Wheeler in the thigh, but Wheeler, the better marksman, struck Tracy four times: in the neck, arm, thigh, and torso. Tracy fell to the ground, feigning surrender and claiming his gun was empty. "My gun is empty, and I am all in."[32]

Since Wheeler did not want to kill Tracy, Wheeler laid his empty gun down before hobbling forward. Except Tracy had only been pretending. With two bullets left, Tracy again opened fire, hitting Wheeler a second time, this time in the left heel. Without a gun, Wheeler resorted to throwing rocks and sticks and anything else at hand while Tracy discharged those last bullets. Wheeler finally reached Tracy, who still refused to hand over his weapon. "We were both very weak, he tried to keep his gun from me (but) bystanders assisted me in taking the gun from him."[33] The reason for Tracy's stubbornness became clear later when extra cartridges were found in his pocket.

Wheeler turned his prisoner over to Deputy Sheriff W. Shillian and sent for Doctors Powell and Morrison. They tended to Wheeler's wounds, then sent him to a hospital in Tombstone where he recovered. Tracy wanted to go to a hospital in Tucson, so they bedded him down on a cot in the baggage car. The train only got as far as Mescal Station, about 10 miles away, before death claimed him. The gallows may have been waiting for him anyway. Tracy had been wanted for two separate murders in Nevada. Officials offered the $500 reward for his capture to Wheeler who refused it and asked that the money be given to the widow of one of the murdered men.

This last case of murder and mayhem exemplifies both the problems created by a transient population and lack of respect for the law. Shortly after midnight on May 10, 1911, Constable Frank Trask was making his rounds in the Southern Pacific yards. As a train began to pull out of a yard, Trask spied a man swing beneath one of the coaches 'to ride the rails' on his way from Tucson to New Mexico.

Trask fired a warning shot into the air to frighten the hobo and get him off the train. Only the hobo wasn't frightened. "...the man demanded of Trask to show his

An artist's rendition of 4th Street with the Virginia Hotel on the right.
The trees would burn in a fire in 1904.
Photo courtesy of Bob Nilson

authority and asked if he was the yard watchman. The officer exhibited his star to the hobo who then remarked, 'You are only a constable here,' and started to run away." Both the *Tombstone Epitaph* and the *Bisbee Daily Review* reported the confrontation with the exact same wording, although it was fairly common for one newspaper to repeat what another newspaper reported.[34]

An earlier article in the *Bisbee Daily Review* claimed that the unknown assailant pulled his gun saying that he "would not be arrested" and opened fire on Trask before he fled. Trask returned the fire although fatally wounded.[35]

There is no question that the hobo fired three shots at Trask hitting Trask in the leg, abdomen, and heart. The shot to the heart proved fatal. Trask also fired at the hobo and hit him through the back into a lung. Although seriously wounded, the hobo fled. The shots, however, had alerted railroad workers who rushed to the scene and captured the hobo who hadn't gotten too far down the tracks because of his injuries.

The hobo was treated on the scene for his wound, then taken to Tombstone. He identified himself as Boyd Smith "...although letters found upon his person give an entirely different name."[36] The court calendar in January 1912 lists "John Smith alias Ryneux charged with the killing of Frank Trask at Benson last summer."[37]

The scenario did raise questions, however, about who fired first. Smith claimed Trask fired at him first and he returned fire in self-defense. Smith was hit in the back—in the act of fleeing. Did he flee after the verbal confrontation and then turn and open fire in response to Trask's shooting at him? Or did Trask manage to get off a round as Smith was fleeing after Smith had fatally wounded him?

Several lawmen had been wounded in Benson, but Frank Trask was "the first Benson lawman to die in the line of duty."[38] His death stirred the community. The *Bisbee Daily Review* claimed that a few "hotheads" wanted to lynch Smith. They did not prevail. By now, 'law and order' had replaced vigilante justice. Until 1924 peace in Benson remained the job of constables, deputy sheriffs, Arizona Rangers, and railroad police.

The bad boys would continue doing their dastardly deeds, of course, as they do in any town or city in any time period. But the wild days of the Old West were drawing to a close as towns grew into permanency with a larger stable population.

# Sources

[1] *Weekly Arizona Citizen.* July 10, 1880.
[2] Ohnesorgen, William. *Reminiscences of an Arizona Pioneer: Personal Experiences of William Ohnesorgen.* Personal interview by Mrs. George Kitt. January 12 (no year given). p. 10.
[3] Palmer, Christena. "The Real Life of Prostitutes in the Old West." www.associatedcontent.com. p. 2.
[4] History\Big Nose Kate, The Shady Ladies, and The 1880's Bordellos. www.bignosekates.info
[5] Sanders, Donnetta C. "White House in Benson Has Bright Purple Past." *The Arizona Republic.* San Pedro Valley Arts & Historical Society. Benson Tidbits, clippings file.
[6] *Arizona Weekly Citizen.* Aug. 21, 1881.
[7] Ibid. Sept. 4, 1881.
[8] Ibid. Sept. 11, 1881.
[9] Sherlock, Basil J. "Community Change in the Southwest: The Case of Benson." *Arizona Review of Business and Public Administration: Bureau of Business and Public Research.* Vol. 12, No. 9. September 1963. p. 3.
[10] "Mansion Hotel Razed." *San Pedro Valley News.* July 9, 1943.
[11] "Benson, June 4, 1882." *Tombstone Epitaph.* June 10, 1882.
[12] Colvin, Clara C. Undated, typewritten document. San Pedro Valley Arts & Historical Society. Benson Tidbits, clippings file.

[13] Blacklidge, Harry J. Letter to Clara Getzwiller dated January 11, 1962. San Pedro Valley Arts & Historical Society. Vertical File: Trask Family. p. 1.
[14] "Filing More Suits." *Bisbee Daily Review.* March 30, 1906.
[15] Becchetti, Fred. Oral history. San Pedro Valley Arts & Historical Society.
[16] McGoffin, Geraldine (Gerry). Oral history. San Pedro Valley Arts & Historical Society.
[17] Myrick, David F. *Railroads of Arizona, Vol. I: the southern roads.* Berkeley, CA: Howell-North Books. 1975. p. 107.
[18] *Arizona Sentinel.* Aug. 27, 1881.
[19] "The Benson Rustlers." *Tombstone Epitaph.* July 29, 1882.
[20] Ibid.
[21] "Benson, June 4, 1882." *Tombstone Epitaph.* June 10, 1882.
[22] A History of Tombstone. www.tombstoneweb.com
[23] "Man Is Killed in Saloon Row." *Bisbee Daily Review.* Dec. 1, 1906.
[24] Ibid.
[25] "A Fatal Shooting," *Graham Guardian.* May 9, 1902.
[26] "Shepard Keeps Still." *Bisbee Daily Review.* May 9, 1902.
[27] "Jury's Verdict." *Bisbee Daily Review.* May 7, 1902.
[28] O'Neal, Bill. *Captain Harry Wheeler: Arizona Lawman.* Austin, Texas: Eakin Press. 2003. p. 41.
[29] Ibid.
[30] "A Fatal Killing." *Tombstone Epitaph.* March 3, 1907.
[31] "Wheeler Gives Statement to Press." *Bisbee Daily Review.* March 6, 1907.
[32] Ibid.
[33] Ibid.

34 "Constable Frank Trask Murdered by a Tramp." *Tombstone Epitaph*. May 14, 1911. (and) "Trask Shot in Air to Frighten Smith." *Bisbee Daily Review*. May 12, 1911.

35 "Deputy Trask Shot by Unknown, Seriously Wounds Assailant." *Bisbee Daily Review*. May 11, 1911.

36 "Constable Frank Trask Murdered by a Tramp." *Tombstone Epitaph*. May 14, 1911.

37 "Court Reconvenes(:) Calendar of Week Is Now Prepared." *Bisbee Daily Review*. January 4, 1912.

38 Benjamin, Stan. *Benson, Arizona: One Hundred Years of Law Enforcement*. Tucson, Arizona: February 2000. p. 4.